What's Your Story?
Seeing Your Life Through God's Eyes
Leader Guide

WHAT'S YOUR Story?

SEEING YOUR LIFE
THROUGH GOD'S EYES

SARAH HEATH

HOW JOSEPH'S STORY
CAN HELP YOU TELL YOURS

LEADER GUIDE

Abingdon Press / Nashville

WHAT'S YOUR STORY?
Seeing Your Life Through God's Eyes
Leader Guide

This book is printed on elemental chlorine-free paper.

978-1-5018-3790-6

17 18 19 20 21 22 23 24 25 26 — 10 9 8 7 6 5 4 3 2 1
MANUFACTURED IN THE UNITED STATES OF AMERICA

Contents

How to Lead This Study

Hello Leader!

Thank you for choosing to lead this exciting study, *What's Your Story? Seeing Your Life Through God's Eyes.* Thank you for taking a chance on this adventure: discovering the story of Joseph and the story of your life, as well as the lives of your fellow study participants, over the next several sessions.

The participant book contains an introduction on the main themes of the study and how it will unfold in each session. But here is a summary of the purpose of *What's Your Story?*: to enable you and your fellow group members to see your lives as stories, written in partnership with God; to help you to see how God is calling you to cowrite this story; and to help you to learn to see these things by exploring them in the story of Joseph (Genesis 37–50).

USING THE PARTICIPANT BOOK

What's Your Story? is divided into four acts. In the participant book, each act includes three sections, beginning with a personal narrative or example, followed by a consideration of how stories are made up, and ending with a reflection on the story of Joseph. Each section of writing is followed by questions to respond

7

to or quotations to ponder, with ample space for participants to interact right in the pages of the book. This is intended as free response space—everyone should feel free to write, draw, color, doodle, or do whatever they like in response to what they find on these pages. Some of the pages call for a specific response, either asking a question or giving instructions. Other pages will simply provide a quotation from the author or another source, and readers will have more freedom in how they respond. By responding to these questions and quotations, participants will have an opportunity to further investigate and contemplate their own stories in relation to what they are learning.

Participants in your group study should plan to read each act in the participant book in advance of your group meeting and should respond to the questions and prompts in the journaling space provided. Your discussions during your group meetings will provide opportunities for you to draw upon and share your responses from the journaling space.

PREPARATION

Each act in this leader guide begins with a summary of the lesson's main ideas, followed by a brief set of instructions and list of supplies that you will need to prepare for your meeting. In addition to reading over these sections of the leader guide, be sure also to read over the lesson plan to familiarize yourself with it. And of course, read the *What's Your Story?* participant book, and respond to the questions and prompts in the journaling spaces in it!

Finally, commit to praying for each of your fellow group members, and ask them to pray for you as well.

MEETING SESSIONS

Determine with your group how often you will meet, and set a time and location. There are four sessions total (with an optional, bonus fifth session if you and your group wish to use it!). Most groups will find it best to meet weekly. Be sure that your meeting space offers a quiet, comfortable spot for discussion and group activities. And be sure that it has a DVD player and television, projector and screen, or computer in order to view the DVD each session. Many groups will prefer to meet somewhere in their church, while others will want to meet in someone's home or at another location each week. Do what works best for your group!

Each session will be structured according to the following lesson plan:

- **Welcome and Opening Prayer** brings everyone together and asks for God's presence and guidance.

- **Begin the Session** opens the lesson with an icebreaker question and an initial discussion of the key ideas for that act of *What's Your Story?*

- **View the Video** gives you a chance to watch the *What's Your Story?* DVD together and discuss the examples it lifts up of the act's key ideas and how they might take shape in someone's life.

- **Engage the Lesson** takes you deeper in your discussion, offers optional activities to help learn the main ideas, and explores the story of Joseph.

- **What's Your Story?** encourages participants to apply what they have learned to their own lives in order to understand their own stories better.

- **Close the Session** allows for any final thoughts to be shared and then brings your meeting to an end with prayer.

There is a suggested time frame for each section, but you should feel free to adjust and adapt the lesson as you see fit. The suggested time frames are based on a meeting that lasts a total of one hour. If you have a longer meeting session, you can easily allow more time for the discussion in any area that you choose.

9

If you have a shorter session, you will likely need to skip parts of the lesson in order to complete it. Most leaders will find it easiest to focus on the discussion in that case and omit the optional activities from the lesson plan.

FLEXIBLE SESSIONS

The lesson plans for each act are designed to be flexible. In each act, you will frequently find two or three questions listed, with instructions to choose one of them and discuss it as a group. This will give you many possible angles from which to approach the lesson and can allow you to chart your own path through the ideas as you study them each week. There are also two or three optional activities to choose from in the Engage the Lesson section, and you are encouraged to choose one of them. Know that you can't go wrong with any of these choices—all of the questions and activities are designed to help you and your group explore and apply the main ideas in a deep, meaningful way. So treat this flexibility as an opportunity for you to choose your own adventure! Have some fun with it, and be open to where your conversations and God's presence lead you each session.

Get ready: you're about to dig deeper into a tale of the ages and follow it all the way through to the story of you.

So let's start this story.

Act One

A Great Story and the Call to Adventure

Scripture: Genesis 37:1-28

Learning Objectives and Main Ideas

- To recognize the importance and power of good stories
- To understand the "hero's journey" as a model for stories and recognize how it can apply to our lives and the story of Joseph
- To describe the character of Joseph in Genesis 37 and understand his Call to Adventure
- To begin seeing our lives as stories, potentially great stories

Prepare

Read act one of *What's Your Story?* by Sarah Heath, and make a note of the main points. In the spaces provided in the book, respond to the questions, quotations,

and other prompts. Identify which ones you would like to use in the group discussion below.

Read over the lesson plan below to familiarize yourself with it, and decide in advance which questions you want to be sure to discuss. Remember, there are several opportunities for you to choose among multiple options. You may choose these in advance, or you may wait and decide when you come to these places based on how your discussion is going.

Decide also which of the three optional activities you wish to use, and gather the supplies you will need for them.

Be sure to have the following supplies on hand:

- Copies of the Bible (multiple translations are OK)
- Pens or pencils for each group member
- A DVD player and television or projector and screen
- The *What's Your Story?* DVD
- A markerboard or large sheet of paper and markers

Welcome and Opening Prayer (1 minute)

Welcome group members as they arrive, and then begin your session with a prayer. Use the one below if you wish, or pray on your own.

Dear God, we know that you are the author of the greatest story ever told, and we know that you are still writing it even today. We want to understand our own stories better and to cowrite them with you. Help us to see your hand at work in the story of Joseph and in our own lives. Amen.

Begin the Session (10 minutes)

Since this is your first meeting as a group, allow the group members to introduce themselves. Choose one of the questions below as an icebreaker. Begin with a volunteer and proceed clockwise until all members have spoken. Invite each member to share his or her name and to answer the question you have chosen:

- Describe one memory from your late teenage years.

- If you had to categorize your seventeen-year-old self as a character, what category would you choose? What role do you think you were playing? (Answers might include the hero or protagonist, the antihero that no one saw coming, the villain or antagonist, the sidekick, or the love interest.)

After everyone has introduced himself or herself and answered the icebreaker question, choose and ask one of the following questions:

- What are the most memorable stories that have formed you in some way? (These may be stories from your childhood that you still remember or ones you encountered later in life.) What is it about these stories that has had such a significant impact on you?

- What was the last book you couldn't put down? What made the book so compelling?

- What is your favorite true story, and how did you encounter it (podcast, radio, documentary, personal conversation, interview, or some other medium)? What drew you in and caused you to connect with this story?

Ask: How did the reflection in act one of *What's Your Story?* help you better understand the makeup of a good story?

All the World's a Stage

The Shakespeare quotation on page 15 of *What's Your Story?*
is taken from the play *As You Like It*, Act II, Scene 7. Shakespeare's
character Jaques asserts that all men are playing out seven stages:
infant, schoolboy, lover, soldier, justice, old age, and imminent death.

The whole quotation is as follows:

All the world's a stage,
And all the men and women merely players;
They have their exits and their entrances,
And one man in his time plays many parts,
His acts being seven ages. At first, the infant,
Mewling and puking in the nurse's arms.
Then the whining schoolboy, with his satchel
And shining morning face, creeping like snail
Unwillingly to school. And then the lover,
Sighing like furnace, with a woeful ballad
Made to his mistress' eyebrow. Then a soldier,
Full of strange oaths and bearded like the pard,
Jealous in honour, sudden and quick in quarrel,
Seeking the bubble reputation
Even in the cannon's mouth. And then the justice,
In fair round belly with a good capon lined,
With eyes severe and beard of formal cut,
Full of wise saws and modern instances;
And so he plays his part. The sixth age shifts
Into the lean and slippered pantaloon,
With spectacles on nose and pouch on side;
His youthful hose, well saved, a world too wide
For his shrunk shank, and his big manly voice,
Turning again toward childish treble, pipes
And whistles in his sound. Last scene of all,
That ends this strange eventful history,
Is second childishness and mere oblivion,
Sans teeth, sans eyes, sans taste, sans everything.[1]

As you discuss the idea of viewing our lives as a story in this session,
you may find it useful to share this information with the rest of the group.

View the Video (10 minutes)

Introduce the video for the group, and prepare to play the *What's Your Story?* DVD. Briefly explain to the group that in each video, author Sarah Heath will introduce the story of one person who illustrates the themes and key ideas of each act in *What's Your Story?* During act one, you'll hear from Mike McHargue, otherwise known as "Science Mike." He's the author of *Finding God in the Waves*, the host of the podcast *Ask Science Mike*, and co-host of *The Liturgists Podcast*. Mike is a Christian who lost his faith and then found it again through science. He's now a leading voice on matters of science and religion.

Play act one of the *What's Your Story?* DVD.

After viewing the video, invite the group to discuss the question Sarah posed at the end. Ask: What is a time in your life when you stepped outside of everything you knew and began an adventure?

Continue discussing the video by asking one of the following questions:

- How did Mike's story illustrate the need to leave the life we know in order to begin a hero's journey? What aspects of his story stood out to you as components of a good story?

- Do you think seventeen-year-old Mike would recognize the Mike of today? What does this say about the nature of our stories?

- How did Mike understand his life as a part of a bigger story? What role(s) in God's story do you think he is playing?

Engage the Lesson (30 minutes)

Invite the group to recall what God's story is about according to act one of *What's Your Story?*

Ask: How does this idea of God writing a story shape your understanding of Scripture? How does it shape your understanding of your own relationship with God?

Choose and ask one of the following questions for the group to discuss:

- Why do you think Jesus told parables? Why did he use stories as a key method of teaching and communicating?

- When you read a story in Scripture, how do you find yourself connecting with it?

- Recall the examples from *What's Your Story?* about non-Christians who are fascinated by the story of Christ. Think also of anybody you know who might be described in this same way. What is it about the Christian story that is so powerful for them? Do you experience the power of the Christian story in the same way?

- Have you ever thought about the Christian liturgical calendar as a way of storytelling? How does this ongoing encounter with the Christian story in worship shape our faith?

Choose one of the following activities to help the group engage and apply the main ideas of this act regarding great stories and good characters.

OPTIONAL ACTIVITY 1:
SHARE YOUR JOURNAL RESPONSES (10 MINUTES)

Invite each person in your group to share his or her responses in the journaling sections of act one of *What's Your Story?* Choose one or two questions or prompts that you found most relevant to the lesson, and ask group members to share their responses to those. Or you may invite group members to share whatever they found most compelling, allowing them to show their work and explain their responses.

Encourage group members to ask questions and comment on one another's responses.

Ask: What new insights into today's lesson do you gain by seeing and hearing the responses of your fellow group members?

Ask: How do they help you in your understanding of your life as a great story?

OPTIONAL ACTIVITY 2:
WORK IN PAIRS (10 MINUTES)

Divide the group into pairs (with one group of three if you have an odd number). Choose one of the questions below, then invite each pair to discuss it among themselves. One partner should respond first; then the second partner should respond. Allow about two minutes per partner, and let the group know when it's time to switch and have the other partner answer.

Invite each partner to answer one of the following questions:

- What is the relationship between your personal, individual story and God's story? Give one specific example to illustrate your point.

- To what extent would you say your individual story is a part of God's story? How do you see God acting within your story, whether outwardly or behind the scenes?

- Think about your life story as a part of God's story. What kind of character are you? What sort of journey or adventure might God be calling you to undertake?

After both partners have responded, bring the group back together. Invite all the pairs to report back about anything interesting they discovered in this process. Say: Based on these discussions, be mindful of how God might be seeking to make your story a part of something bigger!

OPTIONAL ACTIVITY 3:
DISCOVER THE HERO'S JOURNEY (10 MINUTES)

Recall the features of the hero's journey, or monomyth, as discussed in act one of *What's Your Story?* (For further information and background on the hero's journey, visit http://www.thewritersjourney.com/hero's_journey.htm.) Choose one of the stories listed below and outline it using this monomyth structure. If you wish, you may choose instead to outline a story that's not on this list. Ask for a volunteer to map the hero's journey structure visually on a markerboard or large sheet of paper to help guide your discussion.

- The *Lord of the Rings*
- The *Lion, the Witch, and the Wardrobe*
- *Frozen*
- *Star Wars*
- *Cinderella*
- *To Kill a Mockingbird*
- The Parable of the Prodigal Son (Luke 15:11-32)
- The Christian liturgical calendar

Ask: How difficult was it for us to identify the monomyth structure in these stories? What does that say about the nature of our favorite stories and the ways we connect with them?

Ask: How can understanding this structure of so many stories help us understand the story of our own lives?

What Makes a Great Story

On pages 18–21 of *What's Your Story?* you will find a discussion of the work of Joseph Campbell and Donald Miller. Here is some further background on both authors, who have contributed much to our understanding of stories and how we can see our lives as part of God's story.

Joseph Campbell was a hugely influential scholar. His writings about myth have influenced most of the modern landscape of storytelling. After studying many myths and stories from around the world, he noticed that there was a pattern to how captivating stories were structured. Interestingly, just like he noticed in most myth heroes, Joseph himself early on in life had gone on a cross-country exploration to find himself. His first project as a solo author was to write *The Hero with a Thousand Faces*. It outlined the hero's journey, or the monomyth (a word he borrowed from the work of James Joyce, a fellow author). The book has become a classic and is often required reading in courses for filmmakers, historians, anthropologists, and creative writers. The Joseph Campbell Foundation is a great nonprofit resource for information and more learning centered around mythology. On their website, you can hear his lectures and read some of his collected works (http://www.jcf-myth.org).

Donald Miller is a contemporary author who is perhaps best known for his memoir *Blue Like Jazz*. He has found the redemptive value in seeing our lives as stories in some form and has created the Storyline brand around the idea of finding our own story within the grander story of what God is doing in the world. His work has moved beyond just the individual life, and he now works with companies to help them see their own brand as a narrative. For more information on his work, visit www.storylineblog.com.

THE JOSEPH STORY

Transition now to reading the Joseph story using the ideas of story, character, and calls to adventure that you have discussed so far. Choose and ask one of the following questions:

- Do you tend to avoid reading from the Old Testament? Why or why not?

- What do you remember about the story of Joseph? Where did you learn it, and what do you think you'll learn as we read it closely together over the next few weeks?

As a group, read Genesis 37:1-28. You may ask for one or two volunteers to read the whole passage, or you may choose to have several people read three or four verses at a time.

Choose and ask one of the following questions:

- What role does fear play among Joseph's brothers? Can you relate to this fear at all, and if so how?

- What is the difference between Jacob's response to Joseph's dreams and the response of Joseph's brothers? Why do you think we are afraid to look at our own lives with the mind-set Jacob had, a mind-set of "What if...?"

Invite the group to consider the character of Joseph. Ask: How would you describe Joseph's character in this first chapter of the Joseph story? If you had to categorize him as a character type, what category would he fall into?

Ask: What do you see in the biblical text (such as descriptions of Joseph, his speech, his actions) that help you see what his character is like?

Ask: How would you categorize the character of Joseph's brothers? Of Jacob?

Ask: If we consider the Joseph story within the monomyth structure, what part(s) of the structure do you find occurring in this chapter (Genesis 37)? What does that say about where the story will go from here?

The Hebrew Bible
and the Joseph Story

The term *Old Testament* is used within the Christian faith to describe a part of the biblical canon, distinguishing it from the body of writings called the New Testament. The writings of the Old Testament are shared with our Jewish brothers and sisters, and these books make up the full body of Scripture in Judaism. In Judaism, these writings are collectively called the Tanakh, and they are divided into three sections: *Torah* (Law or Instruction), *Nevi'im* (Prophets), and *Ketuvim* (Writings). To call the Tanakh the Old Testament can have negative connotations. It suggests that the books have been replaced by something that is new. *Old* and *new* in our culture tend to be associated with one thing being replaced by something better. To avoid this connotation, in biblical scholarship and in interfaith conversations you will often hear the Old Testament referred to as the Hebrew Bible. This knowledge can be helpful when having interfaith conversations centered around Scripture.

The Joseph story is found in Genesis 37–50, and it tells the story of Jacob's sons. Joseph and his brothers are the sons of Jacob, who is the son of Isaac, who is the son of Abraham. The stories of Abraham, Isaac, and Jacob are told in Genesis 12–36.

What's Your Story? (10 minutes)

Encourage group members to think about their own lives in terms of what we have seen in the Joseph story. Choose and ask one of the following questions:

- When have you had a sense that you were destined for something great? How did other people respond to this sense, or how did you respond to it?

- In your life, when have you felt stuck or forgotten, as Joseph may have felt in the well?

- Imagine yourself in a well right now. What shape does the well take in your life? What circumstances limit you? What seems impossible?

- Name one time in your life when you have felt and responded to a call to adventure. What in your life right now might be another call to adventure?

Ask: What would it mean for you to respond to this situation with a mind-set of "What if…?"

Close the Session (1 minute)

Invite group members to share any final thoughts, then close with a prayer. Use the one below, or pray on your own:

Dear God, we know that you were with Joseph even at the bottom of the well. And we know that you are with us. Open our hearts and minds to the possibility that difficult circumstances might be a call to adventure. In the stories of our lives, shape us as characters who will be faithful to you. Amen.

Remind everyone to read act two of *What's Your Story?* and engage the journaling questions and prompts before your next meeting.

Act Two

The Plot Thickens

Scripture: Genesis 39:1–40:23

Learning Objectives and Main Ideas

- To see plot twists as an integral part of stories and a natural part of life
- To recognize the importance of narrating plot twists, good and bad, within a larger story of one's life
- To discover how painful events or moments in life can become "sacred wounds" that lead to healing for ourselves and others
- To identify the plot twists in Joseph's life in Egypt and how they became an important part of his story

Prepare

Read act two of *What's Your Story?* by Sarah Heath and make a note of the main points. In the spaces provided in the book, respond to the questions, quotations,

and other prompts. Identify which ones you would like to use in the group discussion below.

Read over the lesson plan below to familiarize yourself with it, and decide in advance which questions you want to be sure to discuss. Remember, there are several opportunities for you to choose among multiple options. You may choose these in advance, or you may wait and decide when you come to these places based on how your discussion is going.

Decide also which of the three optional activities you wish to use, and gather the supplies you will need for them.

Be sure to have the following supplies on hand:

- Copies of the Bible (multiple translations are OK)
- Pens or pencils for each group member
- A DVD player and television or projector and screen
- The *What's Your Story?* DVD
- A markerboard or large sheet of paper and markers

Note: You may find the questions in this session a little more intimate in nature compared with those from act one, but as the group spends more time together the questions will get more and more into their stories. Invite them to write down their thoughts in their journals.

Welcome and Opening Prayer (1 minute)

Welcome group members as they arrive, and then begin your session with a prayer. Use the one below if you wish, or pray on your own.

Dear God, thank you for bringing us together. Thank you for always being with us through our plot twists, and grant us the ability to see them and narrate them with courage today. Give us grace to confront our wounds, trusting that they are in your hands and that together with you we can shape them into a healing part of our story. Amen.

Begin the Session (10 minutes)

Begin the session with an icebreaker question, encouraging group members to introduce themselves by name as they respond if new persons are present or if you think it's necessary. Choose and ask one of the questions below. Begin with a volunteer, then proceed counterclockwise (opposite from last time) until everyone has responded.

- Where did you grow up? What do you like most about that place?

- Have you ever had a significant geographical move? What was the biggest thing that changed in your life as a result of the move?

After everyone has responded to the icebreaker question, recall for the group the author's description of the prayer of Jabez on page 40 of *What's Your Story?* Choose and ask one of the following questions:

- What message or messages do people typically hear about negative events or circumstances from the church? How does this compare with the author's understanding of plot twists in *What's Your Story?*

- Do you think our prayers have the power to change God's actions? If so, how should we pray when we are faced with negative circumstances?

The Prayer of Jabez

The prayer of Jabez comes from 1 Chronicles 4:9-10. It is a brief story:

> *⁹ Jabez was more honored than his brothers. His mother had named him Jabez, saying, "I bore him in pain." ¹⁰ Jabez called on Israel's God: "If only you would greatly bless me and increase my territory. May your power go with me to keep me from trouble, so as not to cause me pain." And God granted his request.*

From this Bruce Wilkinson published the book *The Prayer of Jabez*, which suggested that if people would pray this prayer for thirty days they would have great and surprising benefits. Wilkinson was accused by some of subscribing to the prosperity gospel. The prosperity gospel asserts that God wants all of humanity to experience physical and financial prosperity. The idea is that through right belief, positive speaking, and even donations, one's own happiness and prosperity will grow. It suggests that God doesn't want humanity to experience the ups and downs of life, and instead the correct posture toward humanity is one of empowerment and creating happiness. We really don't know much about Jabez or his life, and so it is difficult to know what his motives were and why his prayer was answered.

View the Video (10 minutes)

Introduce the video for the group, and prepare to play the *What's Your Story?* DVD. In this video you'll hear from Jerry Colunga, who experienced a major plot twist when he developed a heart disease as a teenager.

Play act two of the *What's Your Story?* DVD.

After viewing the video, invite the group to discuss the question Sarah posed at the end. Ask: What plot twists have you had in the story of your life?

Continue discussing the video by asking one of the following questions:

- How did Jerry's story illustrate the role of plot twists in a good story or a good life? What did you learn from it about how to respond to plot twists, good or bad?

- What difficult plot twists did Jerry lift up in the video? What role have these played in his life, and how have they shaped his story now?

- What meaning did Jerry find within his plot twists? How does the story he tells help him understand and live with those experiences? What role does God play in the story?

Engage the Lesson (30 minutes)

Encourage everyone in the group to recall the idea of a "sacred wound" from act two of *What's Your Story?* Invite a volunteer to summarize the idea as presented in the book, and then see if any other members would like to add anything to the description.

Ask: How can this idea help us respond to suffering or other challenging experiences? What power or hope do you see in the opportunity to envision wounds and scars as keys to fulfilling the call on our lives?

Choose and ask one of the following questions for the group to discuss:

- When has your sharing of a sacred scar helped others? When have you felt like someone else sharing their pain freed you up?

- Have you ever thought of your greatest wound as a key? What is the wound, and what opportunities for transformation or success might it unlock? Note: People may need some time to think about this question for a bit before answering.

- How did Jesus use people's wounds to minister to them? Where else do you see the idea of sacred wounds in Scripture? What significance do these instances have?

Choose one of the following activities to help the group engage and apply the main ideas of this chapter regarding plot twists or sacred wounds.

OPTIONAL ACTIVITY 1: SHARE YOUR JOURNAL RESPONSES (10 MINUTES)

Invite each person in your group to share his or her responses in the journaling sections of act two of *What's Your Story?* Choose one or two questions or prompts that you found most relevant to the lesson, and ask group members to share their responses to those. Or you may invite group members to share whatever they found most compelling, allowing them to show their work and explain their responses.

Encourage group members to ask questions and comment on one another's responses.

Ask: What new insights into today's lesson do you gain by seeing and hearing the responses of your fellow group members?

Ask: How do these new insights help you in your understanding of your life as a great story?

OPTIONAL ACTIVITY 2:
IDENTIFY SACRED WOUNDS (10 MINUTES)

Act two of *What's Your Story?* describes the character Bilbo in *The Hobbit*, by J. R. R. Tolkien, as an example of a hero with a sacred wound. Bilbo's wound is the fear of being invisible or unhelpful, but he later discovers that invisibility is a key that allows him to help his companions. As a group, spend five minutes thinking of other examples of sacred wounds from books, movies, or real life. Use a markerboard or large sheet of paper to write down all of the ideas you generate.

Record as many instances as you can of heroes with sacred wounds. Be sure to list both the hero and a short description of his or her wound.

After five minutes, invite the group to discuss the following questions:

- What similarities do you find among these heroes and their wounds?

- What relationship do you see between these heroes' wounds and the wounds people bear in our world today?

- How might these stories help you respond to your own wounds or difficult circumstances?

OPTIONAL ACTIVITY 3:
WAYS TO MAKE MEANING (10 MINUTES)

In chapter two of *What's Your Story?*, the author refers to a quotation from Viktor Frankl: "In some way, suffering ceases to be suffering at the moment it finds a meaning, such as the meaning of a sacrifice."[2] Frankl uses the notion of sacrifice as one example of how to make meaning out of suffering. Take five minutes as a group to brainstorm other examples you can think of. Use a markerboard or large sheet of paper to write down all of the ideas you generate. Record as many ways to make meaning out of suffering as you can think of together.

After five minutes, discuss the following questions:

- What is the difference between finding meaning and looking for the positive side? How is finding meaning within suffering more than just finding the silver lining?

- Looking back at your own life or the life of someone you know, where have you seen an attempt to make meaning out of suffering in one of these ways? What hope or healing did it bring?

- How does finding meaning help instances of suffering to become "sacred wounds" through which we discover opportunities to succeed and help others?

Viktor Frankl

Viktor Frankl was an Austrian psychiatrist and neurologist. Frankl, a Jew, was imprisoned and sent to a concentration camp during the Holocaust. While in the concentration camp he noted that those who felt a sense of purpose were able to withstand the huge trauma and not take their own lives. He wrote *Man's Search for Meaning, which was originally titled Nevertheless, Say "Yes" to Life: A Psychologist Experiences the Concentration Camp.* Frankl saw huge success in treating suicidal patients when they were given an opportunity to see their past traumas through a redemptive lens and find meaning in their pain.

Richard Rohr

Fr. Richard Rohr is a Franciscan monk who began the Center of Action and Contemplation. He currently serves as the academic dean of the Living School for Action and Contemplation. He asserts that God is part of us and we are part of God, and because of that we are pushed toward orthopraxis, or right action. He is well known for his prolific writing including *Yes, And...: Daily Meditations; Immortal Diamond: The Search for Our True Self; Falling Upward: A Spirituality for the Two Halves of Life; The Naked Now: Learning to See as the Mystics See;* and *Eager to Love: The Alternative Way of Francis of Assisi.* His writings encourage people to search for their inner selves and lean heavily on mystic teaching. He has been featured in numerous publications and has been a guest speaker for many events, including television appearances on Oprah's Super Soul Sundays.

THE JOSEPH STORY

Transition now to reading and discussing the Joseph story in terms of what you have learned about plot twists thus far. As a group, read Genesis 39:1–40:23. You may ask for two or three volunteers to read the whole passage, or you may choose to have each person read four or five verses and rotate until the whole passage has been read.

Note: If you are pressed for time, you may choose to read only Genesis 39:1-23 out loud and then to summarize the events of Genesis 40 before beginning the discussion.

Choose and ask one of the following questions:

- What changes do you observe in Joseph's character when compared with the passage we read last week (Genesis 37)? To what extent have Joseph's experiences in Egypt led to his development?

- What markers of character do you see Joseph exhibit? How would you characterize him in these passages, and how do his actions or words lead you to this conclusion?

- What might Joseph identify as his sacred wound? If it's somehow a key for Joseph, what might the sacred wound have the potential to unlock?

Invite the group to recall and list all of Joseph's plot twists in Egypt. Choose and ask one of the following questions:

- Is Joseph someone who can't catch a break, or is Joseph someone God continues to bless even through the tough times? What is the difference between these two perspectives? Which do you think Joseph embraces?

- What meaning does Joseph find in each of his plot twists? How might this meaning change over time with each new set of circumstances?

Finish the discussion of Joseph by considering Joseph's decisions in Egypt.

Ask: What choices does Joseph make in Egypt, and how do they contribute to cowriting his story with God?

Ask: What is the relationship between Joseph's choices and the plot twists he has experienced? What does this say about the story God is cowriting with Joseph? with us?

Thoughts in Solitude

The prayer shared at the end of act two is from Thomas Merton, a Trappist monk as well as a well-known author and mystic. He wrote more than seventy books on spirituality and justice and was recognized as a quiet pacifist. This prayer comes from *Thoughts in Solitude*, which reflects on the need for all of us to experience solitude to know ourselves in it. Merton beautifully declares, "Before we can surrender ourselves we must become ourselves. For no one can give up what he does not possess."[3]

What's Your Story? (10 minutes)

Encourage the group to think about their own lives in terms of what you've read and discussed about plot twists and the Joseph story. Choose and ask one of the following questions:

- What are the major plot twists in your life? How have you understood them and responded to them? What sort of story do they seem to be a part of?

- Have you ever felt forgotten or wondered when your time would come? Where do you think God is during times like this?

- How has your suffering put you in a unique position to help others?

Ask: Considering these circumstances we've just discussed, what makes you feel empowered to be a coauthor of your life alongside God? What choices can you make, and how will you receive the results of those choices?

Close the Session (1 minute)

Invite group members to share any final thoughts, then close with a prayer. Use the one below, or pray on your own:

Dear God, our stories, like Joseph's, have plot twists. Help us understand them as a part of life, and help us see the way that you are present within them. Give us the courage and the grace to see them not as something to avoid but as something to make a part of our story. May we find healing from our wounds, and may we bring others to healing as well.

Remind everyone to read act three of *What's Your Story?* and engage the journaling questions and prompts before your next meeting.

Act Three
Embracing Desire and Identity

Scripture: Genesis 41:1-57

Learning Objectives and Main Ideas

- To understand the role that desires play in great stories
- To acknowledge our own desires and discern those which are good and God-given
- To see how Joseph's desires play a role in his climactic moment of standing before Pharaoh to interpret the king's dream
- To recognize our desires and God-given gifts as opportunities for us to cowrite our stories with God

Prepare

Read act three of *What's Your Story?* by Sarah Heath, and make a note of the main points. In the spaces provided in the book, respond to the questions, quotations,

and other prompts. Identify which ones you would like to use in the group discussion below.

Read over the lesson plan below to familiarize yourself with it, and decide in advance which questions you want to be sure to discuss. Remember, there are several opportunities for you to choose among multiple options. You may choose these in advance, or you may wait and decide when you come to these places based on how your discussion is going.

Decide also which of the three optional activities you wish to use, and gather the supplies you will need for them.

Be sure to have the following supplies on hand:

- Copies of the Bible (multiple translations are OK)
- Pens or pencils for each group member
- A DVD player and television or projector and screen
- The *What's Your Story?* DVD
- A markerboard or large sheet of paper and markers

Welcome and Opening Prayer (1 minute)

Welcome group members as they arrive, and then begin your session with a prayer. Use the one below if you wish, or pray on your own.

God, as we continue learning about the Joseph story and the stories of our lives, continue to teach us and give us clarity to understand them. Lead us as we explore our desires and our identity, and help us see how they can become a good part of the story we are cowriting with you. Amen.

Begin the Session (10 minutes)

Begin the session with an icebreaker question. This week, explain to the group that you will choose the first person to respond, and after that person has answered, he or she will choose the next person to respond. Continue in this manner until everyone has answered the icebreaker question. Choose and ask one of the questions below.

- When you were little, what did you want to be when you grew up?

- If you had to choose any occupation (job, career, endeavor, and so on) other than what you're doing now, what would it be?

After everyone has answered the icebreaker question, invite a volunteer to summarize for the group the opening story from act three of *What's Your Story?* about the author's difficulty envisioning a career when she was in college.

Ask: What was the role of desire in the author's ability to determine her vocation? What impact did this have on her sense of identity?

Choose and ask one of the following questions:

- Do you think there is one career path or life path that God has for us, or do you think that we have more freedom in these choices? Which of these answers provides more comfort? More anxiety?

- When have you experienced anxiety about the future course of your life? What role did your desires play in this experience?

- What are the advantages and disadvantages of seeing yourself as a cowriter of your story with God, rather than as a directed playactor? How does this idea change your understanding of your personal story?

Enneagram

One helpful way to discover your deepest desire is to study an Enneagram of your personality. The *Enneagram* is a model of looking at people's primary desire and needs. It helps for understanding our primary motivating forces. It is rooted in many traditions, including Christianity, Judaism, and Islam. These desires, when redeemed, have a positive effect on our story, but when left unchecked, they can turn into vices. Knowing these driving desires can allow God to participate in our continual exploration and healing uses of these desires. A great resource for understanding the Enneagram and how it relates to our faith is *The Enneagram: A Christian Perspective*, by Richard Rohr and Andreas Ebert (Crossroad, 2001). They were some of the first to write a book about the Enneagram in English and have studied the system for many years.

In the Enneagram there are nine personality types, usually defined by the following (adapted from Rohr's and Ebert's book and the Center for Action and Contemplation website): Type one is the "reformer," and the reformer's basic desires are goodness, integrity, and balance. Type one could be described as an idealist. Type two is often known as the "helper," and that person's basic desire is to give and receive love. They often overgive that love or are somewhat resentful for the amount of love they give and can manipulate others by their service. Type three is often described as the "achiever"; the achiever's basic driving desire is to feel valuable. They need constant feedback and successes to help them feel worth. Type four is referred to as the "individualist." Individualists desire most to feel uniquely themselves. They live for beauty and depth. Type five is often called the "investigator." Their basic desire is to understand that which is around them. Investigators are constantly trying to make things clear. Type six is the "loyalist." The deepest need of this type is to have support and guidance. They are afraid of being without that support and require reassurance. Type seven is the "enthusiast," and that person's basic desire is to feel satisfied and content. Their biggest fear is being deprived. Type eight is known as the "challenger," and the challenger's basic desire is self-protection. They are afraid of being harmed or controlled. Those who fall under type nine are known as "peacemakers." Their basic desire is for people to maintain peace and harmony. They truly desire for all to be connected, and understand love as the driving force of all things.[4] Knowing our biggest desires and our biggest fears helps us understand what drives us and what kind of story we can write with God.

View the Video (10 minutes)

Introduce the video for the group, and prepare to play the *What's Your Story?* DVD. In this video you'll hear from Michelle Buessing, whose desires and goals came into focus after a successful battle with breast cancer.

Play act three of the *What's Your Story?* DVD.

After viewing the video, invite the group to discuss the question Sarah posed at the end. Ask: What desires and wants are you working toward, and how can they move your story forward?

Choose and ask one of the following questions to continue discussing the video:

- How did the video describe the relationship between our desires, our identity, and the stories we are living?

- What desires did you see Michelle express in the video? How is her story lived in response to those desires? How have they shaped her identity?

- How did Michelle understand her identity? What are the key roles she plays in life, and how do they shape who she is?

Engage the Lesson (30 minutes)

Invite the group to consider the idea of one's calling or vocation, as expressed in the video and as discussed in the author's experience in act three of *What's Your Story?* Ask: How have you heard the idea of calling being talked about, whether in the church or somewhere else?

Ask: How did the reflection in act three of *What's Your Story?* and the video help you better understand the part that our desires play in determining our calling and cowriting our story? What does this say about how we should respond to our desires?

Choose and ask one of the following questions:

- How have you viewed desires before—bad, good, or neutral? Why? To what extent does this discussion challenge or confirm your view?

- What are the risks and benefits of paying attention to our desires and acknowledging them?

Choose one of the following activities to help the group engage and apply the main ideas of this chapter regarding desires, roles, and identity.

OPTIONAL ACTIVITY 1: SHARE YOUR JOURNAL RESPONSES (10 MINUTES)

Invite each person in your group to share his or her responses in the journaling sections of act three of *What's Your Story?* Choose one or two questions or prompts that you found most relevant to the lesson, and ask group members to share their responses to those. Or you may invite group members to share whatever they found most compelling, allowing them to show their work and explain their responses.

Encourage group members to ask questions and comment on one another's responses.

Ask: What new insights into today's lesson do you gain by seeing and hearing the responses of your fellow group members?

Ask: How do they help you in your understanding of your life as a great story?

OPTIONAL ACTIVITY 2: ADVERTISEMENTS (10 MINUTES)

In act three of *What's Your Story?*, the author notes that our desires don't exist in a vacuum. We are constantly being told what to desire through advertisements, and this can cloud our vision and prevent us from seeing our own good desires clearly. To explore this, encourage everyone to search for advertising messages and pay attention to the ways they are seeking to shape our desires.

Invite each group member to search on his or her smartphone for an advertising message—it can be anything, from a marketing e-mail to a promoted tweet to a video commercial to an advertisement embedded on a webpage. Group members may form pairs or groups of three to work together on this exercise if they prefer. Allow five minutes for this process. Then allow group members to show the advertisement that they have selected.

As an alternative to smartphones, you may bring in magazines and newspapers for the group to search through. Invite individuals to search for advertisements in these publications, selecting one from among what they find.

After completing this exercise, discuss the following questions:

- What were the key objects of desire in these advertisements? Were they the products being advertised or something else?

- What other desires might emerge within us, or become stronger, as a result of this advertisement?

- What desires might be suppressed, or become weaker, as a result of this advertisement?

- What story is this advertisement telling about the people who purchase its product(s) and those who do not purchase its product(s)?

- How does the advertisement seek to write you into that story? How will this affect your own story, which you are cowriting with God?

Skit Variation

As a variation on this exercise, instead of searching individually for advertisements, allow the group to act out a popular commercial in a skit. Divide the group into two teams, and give the teams five minutes to think of a commercial and formulate a plan to act it out. There's only one rule: they can't name the product that's being advertised. Be sure to separate the groups enough so that they can't hear each other talking and planning. After five minutes, invite one team to perform their commercial for the other team, who will try to guess the product that's being advertised. Remember, the team performing can't name the product! After the first team has performed, the second team will perform and the first team will try to guess their product. After both skits have been performed and guessed, discuss the questions above.

OPTIONAL ACTIVITY 3:
ROLES (10 MINUTES)

In act three of *What's Your Story?*, the author says that the many roles we play in life shape our identity. Invite group members to consider what roles they find themselves playing. Make a large number of nametags available, at least ten per person. Explain to the group that you will be thinking about the various roles each of you play in life. Then invite the group members to write down different names on the nametags corresponding to the roles that they live out. Examples might include things like Dad, Mom, Sister, Teacher, Artist, and Friend. As they write each name, they should put on that nametag. By the end, everyone will be wearing many different nametags showing the roles they play.

Note: Group members may have responded to a prompt similar to this activity in the book *What's Your Story?*, in the journal section of act three. If so, this will be a continuation and sharing of what they learned during that experience.

Allow a few minutes for group members to look at one another's nametags, inviting them to ask questions or provide explanations if they so choose. Then discuss using the following questions:

- Do certain roles we find ourselves playing complement or conflict with one another? How should we navigate areas of conflict?

- Is it better to have one strong, primary identity or many identities that contribute somewhat equally to who we are? Why?

- What is the relationship between the roles we play and the desires we have? Which of these, our desires or our roles, contributes the most to our identity? Why?

- As you think about all the roles you play, is there a primary role that you identify with the most strongly? How well does it match the story of your life?

Career and Identity

What we do for work has become a significant identity marker. Major companies aren't just advertising lifestyles, they are also creating workspaces that suggest "What you do for work is who you are." Google, Apple, Netflix, and other famous Silicon Valley employers are making it easy to spend all of your time at your workplace—great perks come with the expectation that you will log long, intense hours at work. There are free meals, free laundry, and even hair salons. You literally could never leave work other than to go home and sleep. Many companies seem to be creating an ethos that we must make our job the central focus of our lives. Author Dorcas Cheng-Tozun writes, "At its best, work connects us to God, gives us meaningful purpose, and provides a conduit for our unique talents and passions."[5] We were never meant to define ourselves by the work that we are engaged in. Our purpose may comingle with our work, but our work is never our purpose.

THE JOSEPH STORY

Transition to reading the Joseph story with the ideas you have discussed so far—desires and identity—in view. As a group, read Genesis 41:1-57. You may ask for one or two volunteers to read the whole passage, or you may choose to have several people read three or four verses at a time.

Choose and ask one of the following questions:

- When have you had to wait a long time for a vision or a dream to come true? What was the experience like, and how did you respond to it? What do you think Joseph was feeling and thinking as he saw an opportunity for greatness in front of him as he stood before Pharaoh?

- Who is the most "important" person you have met? How did you react? What do you think Joseph was going through standing before Pharaoh after such a long time of being imprisoned and experiencing hardship?

- Do you think it was easy for Joseph to trust that what Pharaoh dreamed about would come true? Why or why not?

Ask: What desires does Joseph seem to have as he stands before Pharaoh, and what do you see in the text that tells you this? How is Joseph's meeting with Pharaoh an opportunity to achieve the key desire that's been driving the Joseph story forward?

Ask: How does faithfulness to his own desire contribute to faithfulness to God and to the story that Joseph is cowriting with God?

What's Your Story? (10 minutes)

Encourage group members to think about their own lives in terms of what we have seen in the Joseph story. Choose and ask one of the following questions:

- Joseph has the gift of dream interpretation. What do you think are your gifts? Be bold and name the gifts you have!

- Pharaoh identifies Joseph's talent, saying that there is no one as intelligent and wise as he is. Ask the person to your right to identify the talents that he or she has observed in you over the past few weeks. You might be surprised!

Close by asking the following questions. Allow group members to discuss them if they choose, or simply ask them to ponder them and write the answers in their journals.

- What is the relationship between your gifts and your desires?

- What opportunities might be in your life, waiting on you to act on your desires and trust your God-given gifts?

Close the Session (1 minute)

Invite group members to share any final thoughts; then close with a prayer. Use the one below, or pray on your own:

Loving God, help us to recognize our gifts and the gifts of others, as well as our good desires that honor you. Help us, like Joseph, see opportunities to act on our desires and embrace our gifts, so that we might cowrite the stories of our lives with you. Amen.

Remind everyone to read act four of *What's Your Story?* and engage the journaling questions and prompts before your next meeting.

Act Four

There Is Always Another Act

Scripture: Genesis 42:1–45:15; 50:15-26

Learning Objectives and Main Ideas

- To understand that in life, there is always another act. The story isn't finished.
- To recognize how the Joseph story continues with his brothers after the climax in which he comes to power in Egypt
- To discover opportunities to cowrite with God the next act in one's story

Prepare

Read act four of *What's Your Story?* by Sarah Heath, and make a note of the main points. In the spaces provided, respond to the questions, quotations, and other prompts. Identify which ones you would like to use in the group discussion below.

Read over the lesson plan below to familiarize yourself with it, and decide in advance which questions you want to be sure to discuss. Remember, there are several opportunities for you to choose among multiple options. You may choose these in advance, or you may wait and decide when you come to these places based on how your discussion is going.

Decide also which of the two optional activities you wish to use, and gather the supplies you will need for them.

Be sure to have the following supplies on hand:

- Copies of the Bible (multiple translations are OK)
- Pens or pencils for each group member
- A DVD player and television or projector and screen
- The *What's Your Story?* DVD
- A markerboard or large sheet of paper and markers

Welcome and Opening Prayer (1 minute)

Welcome group members as they arrive, and then begin your session with a prayer. Use the one below if you wish, or pray on your own.

Dear God, thank you for writing such a grand story in this world and for giving us a part to play in it. As we consider our own stories, help us remember that the story is never finished—there is always another act. Help us to find your call to adventure in the next act, so that it might be one in which we partner with you in the story that you are writing. Amen.

Begin the Session (10 minutes)

Begin the session with an icebreaker question. Ask which group member has the birthday earliest in the year (closest to January 1), and have that person respond first. Then ask the person with the next-earliest birthday to respond second.

Proceed in this way until everyone has answered the icebreaker. Choose and ask one of the questions below.

- What is your favorite fairy tale?

- What is your favorite Disney movie?

After everyone has responded to the icebreaker question, explain that most fairy tales, and many Disney movies, end with some version of ". . . and they lived happily ever after." But in act four of *What's Your Story?*, the author observes that real life is never like this. Invite a volunteer to summarize the stories of Ms. Charlotte and uncle Bill from act four. Choose and ask one of the following questions:

- Do you know people who have done many things with their lives? What seems to set such people apart?

- What do you see as the difference between real life and fairy-tale endings? If fairy-tale endings aren't true to life, why are they so compelling and satisfying?

View the Video (10 minutes)

Introduce the video for the group, and prepare to play the *What's Your Story?* DVD. In this video you'll hear from Dan Davidson, a pastor who experienced a climactic moment, only to have things crash down and find that his story continued.

Play act four of the *What's Your Story?* DVD.

After viewing the video, invite the group to discuss the questions Sarah posed at the end. Ask: Has your story developed mostly on the mountaintops, or in the valleys? Why?

Ask: Do our climactic moments turn out to be everything we hope they'll be? How does the idea that life is a series of climactic moments change your view of them?

Continue discussing the video by asking one of the following questions:

- How did Dan's story portray life as an ongoing story that has many new chapters? What did you learn from it that you can apply to your own life?

- What relationship did you see between the various transitions and new acts that Dan lived through? What attitudes, behaviors, or characteristics seemed to emerge no matter what chapter he was in?

- Why did Dan find it meaningful and important to continue living many acts? How did he move forward after one "victory" and on to a new adventure? How did he see God as part of his life throughout each act?

After Achievement

There are many reasons why people have what we might call "post-achievement depression." Usually after achieving something we have worked for with so much focus, we have a huge sense of ecstasy that quickly turns to despair. Why can't we just rest in the achievement? We can't rest because doubt and fear creep in, and we have to be intentional about fighting it off and moving forward. Adele Scheele, who has a PhD in change management and often contributes to *The Huffington Post*, has several suggestions about how to overcome this letdown in her article, "When Success Leaves You Feeling Empty."[6] She suggests keeping a file of past successes to remind you that you have achieved before and will achieve again. She also suggests getting yourself something tangible to look at as a reminder that you have finished something before. (For instance, I just bought that single-lens reflex camera I have always wanted!) The other reason many of us have a sense of depression about achievement is that from a very early age, people have been asking us, "What do you want to do when you grow up?" But that only gives us one option, and once we determine that then we're left feeling goal-less. The truth is we have many potentials. In a fantastic TED talk about this issue, Emilie Wapnick calls us a "multipotentialite." She says that we have a lot of callings on our lives.[7] The key is living faithfully into all of these callings as we cowrite our story!

Engage the Lesson (30 minutes)

Invite everyone in the group to recall the notion of finding a new call to adventure or inciting incident in one's life from act four of *What's Your Story?* Select a volunteer to summarize these ideas for the group.

Ask: How can calls to adventure or inciting incidents create movement in our stories? What do these things accomplish for us? Is it possible to create a call to adventure for yourself? Why or why not?

Choose and ask one of the following questions for the group to discuss:

- Is there some goal or vision that you keep putting off (e.g., getting in shape, getting in contact with a friend, starting a new project)? What movement could you begin today toward this goal?

- What calls to adventure do you think have created movement in your story? What might be calling you into the next act?

- What is one of your greatest achievements, or what felt like a pinnacle moment in your life? How did you feel after this moment? How did you decide what life would look like after it?

Choose one of the following activities to help the group engage and apply the main ideas of this chapter about stories that continue into new acts.

OPTIONAL ACTIVITY 1:
SHARE YOUR JOURNAL RESPONSES (10 MINUTES)

Invite each person in your group to share his or her responses in the journaling sections of act four of *What's Your Story?* Choose one or two questions or prompts that you found most relevant to the lesson, and ask group members to share their responses to those. Or you may invite group members to share whatever they found most compelling, allowing them to show their work and explain their responses.

Encourage group members to ask questions and comment on one another's responses.

Ask: What new insights into today's lesson do you gain by seeing and hearing the responses of your fellow group members?

Ask: How do they help you in your understanding of your life as a great story?

OPTIONAL ACTIVITY 2: THE DAY AFTER HAPPILY EVER AFTER (10 MINUTES)

Divide the group into two teams. If your group is larger, you may wish to divide into three or more teams. Ask each team to choose a fairy tale. They can choose any fairy tale they like—the only requirement is that every team member must know the story, and it must end in "...and they lived happily ever after."

Explain to the teams that they will have seven minutes to write the next act in the fairy tale—what comes after "happily ever after." Instead of beginning with "once upon a time," the next act should begin, "The day after happily ever after...." Each team should first think of a single call to adventure or inciting incident to begin this next act and then write the rest of the story from there. Encourage the groups to apply everything they have learned about stories from *What's Your Story?* so far.

Allow five minutes for the teams to work, then call time. Invite a storyteller from each team to relate the name of the team's fairy tale, then tell the story of the next act, beginning with "The day after happily ever after..."

After each team has told their story, discuss one of the following questions:

- How did what happened in the original fairy tale influence what happened in the next act?
- What climax did the next act move toward? What was the relationship between this and the original fairy tale?

Conclude by asking: How does adding the next act to the fairy tale change the story? What can you learn from this about how we should live the next act in our own stories?

OPTIONAL ACTIVITY 3: SHARE YOUR STORIES (PLAN A FOLLOW-UP GROUP SESSION)

Instead of a third optional activity for this session, instructions are provided for your group to plan an extra, optional follow-up session in which you share your stories with one another. See the instructions beginning on page 61.

THE JOSEPH STORY

Transition now to reading and discussing the next act of the Joseph story, in which Joseph encounters his brothers again after two decades of separation. Invite one group member to read Genesis 42:1-16. Then ask another group member to summarize what happens next as Joseph and his brothers continue to interact.

Ask a third volunteer to read Judah's speech to Joseph in Genesis 44:18-34. Finally, ask a fourth volunteer to read Genesis 45:1-15, where Joseph reveals his identity to his brothers.

Choose and ask one of the following questions:

- How would you have responded if you were in Joseph's shoes and saw your brothers for the first time since they sold you into slavery?
- What do you think about the tests Joseph put his brothers through? How do you think the brothers felt, and what might Joseph's reasons have been for treating them this way?
- What seems to have changed in the brothers? What seems to have changed in Joseph? What do you see in the biblical passages that alerts you to these changes?

Invite the group to recall the scenes of Joseph's forgiveness in Genesis 45 and 50. Then discuss one of the following questions:

- What is at stake in Joseph's decision to forgive, or not forgive, his brothers? How would choosing not to forgive them have held Joseph back?

- What is Joseph's primary motivation for forgiving his brothers? How does his choice to forgive them affect their story going forward?

- Why do you think the brothers struggle to accept and trust Joseph's forgiveness? What will need to change within them or about them in order for them to trust him going forward?

Ask: How do our relationships with other people factor into the next acts in our personal stories? How do our decisions about these relationships shape the way our stories move forward?

What's Your Story? (10 minutes)

Encourage the group to think about their own lives in terms of what you've read and discussed about the next act of the Joseph story. Choose and ask one of the following questions:

- Is there a chapter of your life that you struggle to move on from, like Joseph's brothers seem to have experienced? What can you do to envision new possibilities?

- As you look toward the challenges and opportunities in your own life, what potential do you see for the next act of your story? How will your decisions affect the way this story plays out? What does God seem to be calling you to do?

Encourage the group to think through everything they have learned over the course of your time together.

Ask: Name one thing that you have learned over the last several sessions. How will it impact the way you understand your story?

Ask: How will you let God be your coauthor? How will you make yourself available to be God's coauthor? What's next in your story?

Close the Session (1 minute)

Invite group members to share any final thoughts, and thank them for their contributions over the course of your study. Make plans to follow up with anyone who might be interested. Then close with a prayer. Use the one below, or pray on your own:

Dear God, we are grateful for all the things you have shown us throughout this study. Thank you for helping us understand the power of good stories and the power of reading our lives as good stories. Thank you for helping us understand the Joseph story more deeply and for the insights we have gained into our own lives as a result. Most of all, thank you for the ways in which we have felt you leading us to embrace new opportunities and new calls to adventure. May we cowrite with you great stories and be great characters within those stories. Amen.

Bonus Session:
What's Your Story?

Note: If you are doing the bonus session, make sure to prepare people by asking them to write out their stories in advance, using the time line they created on pages 44–45 of *What's Your Story?* and Joseph Campbell's idea of the hero's journey. Be sure to do this for your own story as well!

Welcome and Opening Prayer (1 minute)

Welcome group members as they arrive, then begin your session with a prayer. Use the one below if you wish, or pray on your own.

Dear God, thank you for coauthoring with us. Remind us of your presence through-out our story. Today as we share or as we hear others share our stories, may we feel a sense of connection to one another and to our stories. Help us to feel bold in sharing, and remind us that no one chapter defines our entire story. Amen.

Begin the Session (2 minutes)

Share with people that today is a special closing day for your group and that for those who feel empowered, there will be an opportunity to share their story.

Make sure that you set a time limit based on the number of participants and amount of time you have scheduled for the class.

View the Video (10 minutes)

Play the bonus session of the *What's Your Story?* DVD.

Say: "At the end of the video, Sarah told us that we have a powerful story to tell. So let us enter into a time of sharing our stories."

Invite each participant who feels comfortable to share his or her story. Encourage the group to listen for themes, and make sure each person is encouraged after telling the story. If your group is large, have people break up into smaller teams and share their stories with the others in their team.

Close the Session (1 minute)

Invite group members to share any final thoughts, and thank them for their contributions over the course of your study. Make plans to follow up with anyone who might be interested. Then close with a prayer. Use the one below, or pray on your own:

Dear God, thank you for this time of hearing one another. May we begin to view our own stories as powerful and transformational not just for ourselves, but for others. May we take time to reflect as we continue to live this hero's journey, looking for places where you are inviting us to live lives of great adventure. Thank you for everyone who shared today, and thank you for a community that could receive their stories. May you continue to write alongside all of us and whisper in our ears calls of adventure all the days of our lives. Amen.

Notes

1. William Shakespeare, *As You Like It*, II.vii.139–66, accessed January 2, 2017, https://www.poets.org/poetsorg/poem/you-it-act-ii-scene-vii-all-worlds-stage.

2. Viktor E. Frankl, *Man's Search for Meaning* (Boston: Beacon, 2006), 113.

3. Thomas Merton, *Thoughts in Solitude* (New York: Farrar, Straus and Giroux, 1999), 18.

4. For more information and helpful resources, visit www.cac.org/the-enneagram -an-introduction/.

5. Ibid.

6. Adele Scheele, "When Success Leaves You Feeling Empty," *The Huffington Post*, January 26, 2012 (updated March 7, 2012), accessed January 2, 2017, http://www.huffingtonpost.com/adele-scheele/managin-success_b_1234588.html.

7. Emilie Wapnick, "Why Some of Us Don't Have One True Calling," TED Talk, TEDxBend, April 2015, accessed January 2, 2017, https://www.ted.com/talks/emilie_wapnick_why_some_of_us_don_t_have_one_true_calling.

CPSIA information can be obtained
at www.ICGtesting.com
Printed in the USA
LVOW13s0529140317
527078LV00004B/6/P